Family Vacations that Work

TIM HANSEL

LIFEJOURNEY
BOOKS

LifeJourney Books is an imprint of David C. Cook
Publishing Co.
David C. Cook Publishing Co., Elgin, Illinois 60120
David C. Cook Publishing Co., Weston, Ontario
Nova Distribution, Ltd., Torquay, England

Family Vacations That Work
©1991 by Tim Hansel

(This booklet consists of selected portions of *When I
Relax, I Feel Guilty* ©1979 by Tim Hansel)

Edited by Brian Reck
Cover design by Bob Fuller
First printing, 1991
Printed in the United States of America
95 94 93 92 91 5 4 3 2 1

Library of Congress Cataloging in Publication Data
Hansel, Tim
Family Vacations that Work/Tim Hansel
    p. cm. — (Helping Families Grow series)
ISBN: 1-55513-607-9
1. Family recreation. 2. Vacations—Planning
I. Title   II. Series:
GV182.8H36 1991
790.1'91—dc20   91-27591
                                            CIP

*If happiness could be found in having material
things, and in being able to indulge yourself in
things that you consider pleasurable, then we,
in America, would be deliriously happy. We
would be telling one another frequently of our
unparalleled bliss, rather than trading tranquil-
izer prescriptions.*   John Gardner
                                                Self-Renewal

Any idea that is not a little dangerous is
probably not worth being called an idea. As
A. N. Whitehead said, "It's the business of
the future to be dangerous." This is the
dangerous part of this booklet.

The real test of this booklet is not just whether or not you like it, but whether you are willing to do something about it. The acid test occurs when you lay this booklet down.

It seems to be getting easier and easier these days to thrive on the vicarious experience of others—through spectator sports, TV dramas, personality magazines, and yes, even books. But secondhand experience results only in dissatisfaction. The more we experience life directly, the deeper our joy. One of the greatest insults we pay God is to say we are bored.

What can we do to start living life directly? The following pages will offer some specific suggestions. We'll start with perhaps the most familiar form of leisure—the vacation.

VACATION KILLERS

"Having a lousy time. Wish I weren't here." Why are so many vacations losers? Some people experience disappointment year after year and never know why. Here are a few thoughts that might help.

Don't overwait. Some people demand a reason for everything, and thus don't take a vacation until they desperately need one—when they are physically and emotionally exhausted, or ill. Even a trip to Paradise would be hard pressed to make up those odds.

Don't overdo. Since they've waited fifty weeks for this vacation, some people try to cram a year's worth of living into two weeks. They wind up pushing harder and spending longer hours than they do on the job. Rushing from one place to the next, "hurrying to be happy," it's no wonder that peace eludes them.

Don't overexpect. Related to this image that vacation is a reward for hard work is the notion that therefore we are supposed to enjoy this time, and if we don't, we feel anxious. We carry so many bionic images of leisure into the vacation that nothing could ever match it—and then wonder why we're so unhappy.

To anticipate that a place can make you happy because a full-page ad says it can is inviting a letdown. Likewise to be impatient because your last purchase didn't make you ecstatic is sheer nonsense. Yet each day, more of us slide into this subtle trap, mainly because we don't want to be responsible for our own enjoyment. We want to pay someone else to make us happy. But it doesn't work that way. Joy must spring from within.

How do we begin to bring more life into our leisure, and particularly our vacations? One of the biggest steps is recognizing that we might have some difficulties with leisure time. A large part of the solution to any problem lies in an honest recognition that it exists. This awareness may lead to a change in behavior, and that prospect may be a little frightening. But the risk is worth taking. What specific steps might help if you are the victim of vacation blues?

VACATION CHECKLIST

1. *Have reasonable expectations* rather than impossible ones, ones that invariably lead to disappointment. A vacation will not necessarily make you a new person or salvage a troubled marriage. But it can, and will, be refreshing—if you let it be.

2. *Examine some of your past vacations.* Be objective, but be compassionate. Don't vilify yourself, no matter how your past trips have turned out. Just try to think of ways they could be improved.

3. *Relax.* Don't hurry past the beauty. Joy is a gentle and delicate living thing. Let it happen.

4. *Don't take yourself too seriously.* Expect some obstacles. Embrace them. Even laugh at them if you can. Convert them into part of your vacation. Make an adventure out of your inevitable mishaps. Murphy's Law—which say that if anything can possibly go wrong, it will not only do so, but at the worst possible time—still has a habit of inviting itself on a lot of vacations. Don't let it ruin yours.

5. *Be creative.* Put a little variety into your celebrations. Don't let someone from a travel agency plan your happiness. Let your imaginative juices flow. Make each vacation a once-in-a-lifetime experience.

6. *Take all of you on vacation.* Use all of your senses. This is a time when you can be whole, when you can use your smeller for something more than just to keep your hat off your shoulders. Don't just eat; taste your food. Let your vacation be a five-sense event.

7. *Plan a strategy for vacation diet.* Enjoy your food, but don't make it the whole purpose of your vacation. Resistance is usually a little lower during vacations.

Fatigue, frustration, or even boredom sometimes stimulate indulgence. Have a plan.

" 'By golly,' shouted Lizzie's husband, as he pushed the third brioche of the continental breakfast under her nose while vacationing in Paris, 'we're paying for it, we're gonna eat it.' Normally Lizzie's breakfast at home amounted to 200 calories. Her vacation breakfast that day: 1,000 calories."[1]

Without some forethought, overeating can ruin a vacation. Take low-calorie snacks for those long rides in the car, and remember that the famous response to why something was done—"because it's there"—was meant for climbing mountains, not eating.

8. *Get regular exercise.* Not only will this help you control your diet, but it will also help you enjoy your trip. A good balance between rest and activity is best.

9. *Take short vacations* if long ones make you homesick, especially if you are taking one of those special getaways without the kids. But make sure you give yourself enough time to unwind fully.

10. *Forget such maxims as "Hard work deserves a rest."* Don't spend all your time justifying your vacation. A vacation isn't

just a dessert for a job well done. Enjoy it for what it is—time to live.

11. *Break your routine.* Get up at a different time than you usually do during the year. If you never get to read—read. If you read as part of your job— put down the books for a few weeks. Let some new light into your life.

12. *Do something unusual.* Be an experimenter. Meet new people, try new experiences. Let people think you're loony. Wear a funny hat or put your shirt on backwards for a day. Roller-skate down a shopping mall. Climb a mountain, or a tree. Don't wear a watch for a week. Hug a tree, fly a kite, wear a button, jog in triangles. Fool somebody. Fool two somebodies. Go for a long walk in your barefeet. Poke some holes in your rigidity. This is not a time to be timid. Take a chance. It's worth it.

13. *Do something a little extravagant.* Buy something you've always wanted. Let go a little bit. Don't be so reasonable all the time.

14. *Learn something new on your vacation.* One of the great joys in life is learning. Teach yourself to play chess, or learn to needlepoint. Learn calligraphy and send fancy postcards to all your friends. Uncover

some of those talents you've been hiding.

15. *Learn to look for the best and laugh at the worst.* You will usually see what you are looking for. Choose to see the good, the best, the beautiful. Also choose to laugh at the crazy things that always want to go on vacation with you—flat tires, flat hair, flat spirits, flat experiences. A couple summers ago when melting ice caused a river to flood our campsite, a friend woke me with the comment that "the dew was a little heavier this morning." No one can make you depressed but yourself.

16. *Give yourself permission to be happy.* Practice it. Work hard to eliminate that free-floating guilt that still says you should be working or doing something more useful, and that you shouldn't be having such a good time. Let your restless spirit relax for a few moments. Let your cup overflow. Fruit is simply the excess of life. You can't try to bear fruit; you've got to let it happen.

17. *Let the hero out in you.* Live each day and each vacation as if it were your last opportunity. Rejoice and crack the skies with laughter. Let your passion for being alive and being one of God's people encourage you to be the very best you can be. Put

forth the best qualities of your personality to each person and each situation you meet—and in giving it away, much of it will contagiously rub off on you.

IDEAS FOR ACTIVE REST

"Why did Mister God rest on the seventh day?" she began.

"I suppose he was a bit flaked out after six days hard work," I answered.

"He didn't rest cause he was tired, though."

"Oh, didn't he? It makes me tired just to think about it all."

"Course he didn't. He wasn't tired."

"Wasn't he?"

"No, he made *rest."*

Fynn
Mister God, This Is Anna

Vacations don't have to be escapes— they can be introductions. They shouldn't always be vacations from something (a vacation from the kids, from the routine, etc.). Perhaps what you need is a vacation *to*. This booklet will describe some unusual ideas for vacations both *to* and *from*.

Vacation designs need to vary according to your purpose. Before your start planning your next vacation, you should know (1) what your particular needs are at this time in your life (rest? activity? change of scenery? solitude?) and (2) what your hopes are. Then these factors should be woven together as you create your living vacation.

VACATIONS *TO*

A vacation *to* is a purposeful exploration of varying length (from a few hours to a few weeks) of a specific idea that appeals to you. Some of the things you must remember are to travel light, don't spend all your time driving, have a specific purpose in mind (even if it's being "nonpurposeful" for a few hours), be a little daring, and enjoy it with all your senses. Here are a few ideas to get you going:

1. *Health vacations.* If you're feeling a little sluggish, maybe you need to spend some time focusing on yourself and your health. As Anna said, "And we're out to love God with all our hearts, to love our friends, and don't forget to take some time to love ourselves."[2] Love yourself by taking some days to develop some solid health patterns. It may be a tennis vacation, a jogging vacation on the coast, a cycling vacation to visit some friends, or a hiking

vacation in the mountains. Work on filling your lungs with a lot of oxygen, your mind with a lot of good thoughts, and your body with a lot of good food.

2. *Educational vacations.* Have you ever thought of taking some vacation time with the specific intent of learning something new? You may want to learn how to fix a car, or do woodwork, or rock-climb. You may go somewhere to learn how to paint or cook, or set aside special time at home to take classes at a local college.

3. *Back-roads vacations.* Some friends recently spent their entire vacation on back roads. What stories they had to tell about friendly people they met and unusual places they saw. Part of the adventure was in planning how to get there using only back roads; the other part was enjoying all the serendipitous events that naturally happen on such a trip.

4. *Children's vacations.* Let your children plan and, as much as possible, implement a short vacation. It might be very exciting seeing the world from their eyes. Stay flexible, and plan on a lot of surprises.

5. *Cheap vacations.* These can be some of the most inventive kind ever. The purpose

here is to discover how much you can do with as little money as possible (many of you have had a lot of practice already). For example, how many things can you do for twenty-five cents? How about one dollar? What can your whole family do for five dollars? Look in the newspapers for all the free films and exhibits you can go to. List all the places you can explore for nothing. There are more than you might normally think. Keep a scrapbook of ideas, or put them on your bulletin board in bright and funny colors. How far can you travel on seventy-nine cents? How creative are you at eating for a day on $1.12? The ideas are endless—and the results in joy and how you feel about yourself are worth more than the money you save.

6. *Sunset Magazine vacations.* Many of us want our houses to look like *Better Homes and Gardens* instead of *Popular Mechanics,* but we need time to develop ideas that will fit our particular Quonset hut. Why not take the time? Set aside time with the fixed aim of getting ideas (and having fun). Leave the children home this time and go see different kinds of architecture, color patterns, fences, and porch designs. Then

take a sketch pad and talk of all the wild possibilities over dinner. If you have a lot of good ideas, go to a motel for an evening and continue the conversation.

7. *Reinventory vacations.* Has it ever occurred to you to take time to remember what is special to you? We can get so busy that we forget what's really important. What about taking an overnight vacation, or maybe a weekend, and resolve to redefine your values (and try to figure out how to implement them)?

Start with your lifetime goal. Do you know what it is? Do you know it with enough clarity to write it down? What are some of your lifetime dreams? Your priorities? Are you living in accordance with them these days? How could you improve? It's important to be specific.

Take whatever resources along with you that you might need (Bible, writing material, tapes, other books, etc.), but don't forget that unhurried and uncrowded time will be your most important resource.

8. *Memory lane vacations.* Revisit some of those special places that have been hallmarks in your life. Take the time to see old friends. Spend some evenings remembering, laugh-

ing, telling stories, and maybe even going through some of the old annuals. Relish the nostalgia for a while.

9. *Evangelistic vacations.* Bill and Carolyn Young recently took a delightful vacation to Oregon, where their distinct purpose was to share their faith in Jesus Christ. In doing so they revitalized not only the lives of a lot of other people but their own as well. Their relationship grew stronger because they really needed each other, and their faith grew because of the challenge.

10. *Just Being vacations.* Take off your watch for a while. Forget what time it is. Eat when you're hungry instead of at noon. Reestablish your relationship with God, with your lifetime companion, and with yourself on the basis of who you are rather than what you do.

Pam and I were sharing a weekend like this in the mountains last year at a friend's cabin when I looked over and noticed that the alarm clock had no hands. It was nice to think that nothing could alarm us, and that we had discovered, at least for a while, some untime. Untime like this can be dictated by spontaneity. Travel very light, plan very little, lead with your heart, and let life surprise you around every corner. Leave spacious "do nothing time" for doing what you feel like. Take long "nothing walks" for the sole purpose of enjoying the walk. Get in touch with your feet and your body again. Read fairy tales and poetry, take naps, and realize that you are, and that that is enough.

11. *Vacations you train for.* This summer my wife and I are planning to ride our bikes in southern Oregon for a specified distance. Part of the joy has been in the training necessary—we're training for a purpose. Select a purpose and make a vacation out of getting ready for it.

12. *Seeing vacations.* Have you ever thought of deliberately spending some days (either at home or traveling) to discover the magic of seeing? We take our eyes for granted so often and use them just to keep from bumping into things. Said Helen Keller, "I have walked with people whose eyes are full of light but who see nothing in sea or sky, nothing in city streets, nothing in books. It were far better to sail forever in the night of blindness . . . than to be content with the mere act of looking without seeing."[3]

See color, for example. Follow one color for the whole day. You will be amazed at how much you've been blind to. Sit quietly on the grass and allow your eyes to marvel at the world around you. A bush, a cloud, or a leaf might become an unforgettable experience. Draw a circle about six feet in diameter around you and see as many things as you can within that "magic circle." Your eyes will never be the same.

We do a lot of looking everyday: through lenses, telescopes, television tubes. We look more and more, but see less and less. Unless we slow down to see more than just labels and directions, we become merely spectators, and in the Kingdom of God no one can see as long as he remains just a spectator.

Seeing vacations can be expanded upon. Take along a camera, and photograph the splendor you see. If you like, choose to focus on seeing and photographing faces for a day. Another possibility is to take a pencil and sketch pad, and explore your artistic talents. Drawing, says Frederick Franck, is the discipline by which he constantly redis-covers the world. You can't beat that for a vacation.

13. *A wonder trip.* As you did with seeing, now explore the magnificence of life

with all your senses. Unwrap some of the incredible gifts of life around you. There is so much more there than normally meets the eye. Take time to ask questions rather than seek answers. How does grass grow up through cement? How does a bird fly? How do grunion know to ride the high tide? There are thousands of questions, which, like treasure chests, are waiting for your exploration. As Thomas Carlyle said, "The man who cannot wonder is but a pair of spectacles behind which there is no eyes."[4]

14. *Gourmet vacations*. Rediscover that food is something more than stuffing. Turn an evening into a mini-vacation by immersing yourself without inhibition into the life of a gourmet. Dress in your fanciest. Eat very slowly, tasting every morsel. Feast on the candlelight atmosphere as well. Ask the waiter complex questions on how the food was prepared—and then take a menu home for memories.

15. *Change of life-style or service vacations*. Not all leisure has to be leisure to be enjoyable. What about taking your family to the midwest to work on a farm, or to help friends build a house? What about arranging a long trip with a truck driver you

know? Or volunteering your services at a hospital or a convalescent home? Albert Schweitzer said late in his life, "The only ones among you who will be truly happy are those who have sought and found how to serve."

16. *Exploration vacations.* Your only limit here is creativity. Explore a friendship through traveling together on a vacation. Explore a book or an idea. Jack Meyer, a very special friend of mine, has devoted this year to studying the thought of C. S. Lewis. He is pursuing—through reading, travel, discussion with friends, media, and any other source of information—to know and understand this great Christian thinker.

17. *Once-in-a-lifetime specials.* There are so many things to do that we will probably do only once. Design a day around going for a ride in a helicopter, or going to a horse race. Find a bookbinder and find out how books are bound. Take a weekend to go skydiving or shoot the rapids. Do something a little eccentric, like going to an umbrella factory or following the whole process behind the making of toilet paper. It might be great fun—and will probably be a terrific conversation stopper at your next party.

18. *One parent, one child occasions.* Make a midget vacation out of spending quality time alone with one of your children. It can just be dinner together, or it can be a whole weekend trip. You might participate in an event together or explore an idea together. (If she's younger, you might have a little vacation "learning to be a lady.") A father-son rock climbing venture, where each has to belay the other on the end of a rope, might introduce lifelong qualities to the relationship.

19. *Rest vacations.* In an article entitled "How to Conquer the Spiritual Blahs," Bill Bright focused at one point on the spiritual problems that have their source in sheer physical fatigue. Some of us need the kind of vacation that has rest as its undeviating purpose. Go somewhere where no one can find you, take the phone off the hook, and spend most of the days horizontal. Give yourself permission to get recharged. Give your body a breather. It could be the vacation that will get you prepared for the rest of your vacations.

20. *The third honeymoon.* Have you taken time to experience your second honeymoon yet? If not, you'll have to do that first. The

purpose of honeymoon specials is to take time to remember who you are married to, and why. If you have a copy of your wedding vows, bring them along and reread them. If not, maybe you'll want to start your little rehoneymoon after attending the wedding of some friends. Maybe you will take time to write new vows that pertain especially to your commitment to each other during the second season of your marriage.

Other ideas include such things as going back to the place where you had your original honeymoon, making something special for each other with your hands, framing some of the special photos from your marriage and honeymoon, reading a book out loud together, having something special engraved for the one you love, spending an afternoon or evening together, writing a journal of all the special events in your marriage, writing a poem together, and writing down ten things you'd like to do together in the next year.

As you can see, ideas for bringing more variety and fulfillment into your life through vacationing are plentiful. Obviously, there are many, many more. Maybe one of your family mini-vacations could be a brainstorming session to list the ones not touched upon here—such as historical vacations, underwater vacations, a "Roots" vacation, primitive vacations, and the like.

VACATIONS *FROM*

Not only are there vacations that have a distinct purpose of going *to* something, but there can likewise be a rainbow of possibilities of important vacations *from* something. Consider, if you will, some of the following twenty-four-hour vacations from aspects of life that might limit you in some way:

1. *Vacation from words.* A twenty-four-hour mini-vacation from words might not only be very peaceful, but might also bring new insight into their value. We speak, as I understand it, more than five thousand words in a day. A quiet revolution might occur if we didn't have them for a day.

2. *Vacation from food.* It's commonly called a fast, rather than a vacation—but who says you can't change your attitude to make it a celebration rather than an endurance contest? It's one of the most important little vacations I know. If done with regularity, it will change not only your weight, but also your life-style.

3. *A vacation from seeing or hearing.* Some years ago I taped my eyes for a good part of a week so that I was totally blind. That time probably taught me more about my senses than any five books could have done. It was the first time I realized that my nose could do more than get broken. I did it with a friend who served as my guide. Dick was an aggressive learner and teacher, so he had me do things like go running with him, jump off a fifteen-foot tower into a lake, write a letter, and find my way out of the woods alone—so my experience was enhanced greatly. Since then I've intention-ally limited other senses in order to isolate and experience them. They have all been priceless life investments.

4. *Vacation from complaining.* One of the assignments I frequently give my students is to try to go twenty-four hours without complaining. It is undoubtedly one of the toughest assignments they have during the entire year. No one has successfully made it yet— but the experience of trying it is poignant, painful, and enlightening. Few of us are aware of the extent of our complain-ing. Attempting such a "vacation" will bring you to your knees in humility. Have some

friends do it, too, the same day. Take notes during the day of your experiences, and then get together later to discuss it. It may bring about some important changes.

Not all of these mini vacations have to be limited to twenty-four hours. You may want, for example, to take a one-week to six-month vacation from your television just to learn more about its influence in your life. You may choose to design a vacation from your telephone for a period of time. Some have decided to take a vacation from meat or sugar. The joy and the challenge is again twofold—first, to diagnose those things that you may feel to be keeping you from your best, and second, to design a creative and pleasant mini vacation.

IDEAS FOR MAXI AND MINI VACATIONS

If I am content with little, enough is as good as a feast.—Isaac Bickerstaff

Have you ever thought of taking a two-minute vacation? "Too short," you say? Guess again.

What about a three-year vacation? Too long? Too impractical? It all depends on how you view the word *vacation*.

Who ever said all vacations had to be two weeks long? Breathe some fresh air into your thinking. As varied as the types of vacations are their potential lengths.

If you are "vacating" only once a year (the usual thought pattern), that two-week block of time almost suffocates in the desperate attempt to do a whole year's worth of living in that time. Putting all your vacational eggs in one basket is ineffective and usually leads to depression. We would do much better to plan more consistent and more frequent breaks, each with a different purpose, to meet the various needs of our family.

SUPER-MAXI VACATIONS

A super-maxi vacation experience is the fruit of a lot of planning, togetherness, and courage. It's not really a vacation—it is a family experience that combines all their vacation thoughts for the year. No one I know of can afford six months to a year off, but most families could draw together what might be called "a string of pearls." This is an extended, full-bodied, sometimes challenging, sometimes relaxing warehouse of opportunities bound together not only by the participants but also by a theme of what you've chosen to do. It might be, for example, that you decide the year will be the "Year of Adventure." You might do such things as learn how to sail, rock-climb, sky-dive, and do karate during the course of that year. Or you could take on an adventure of the mind or spirit like learning how to meditate on Bible passages. Other possibilities include taking a year to simplify your life-style, or devoting a year to developing spartan health habits, or learning to build grandfather clocks.

MAXI VACATIONS

Some people have jobs that give them extended periods off. Usually these individuals are rather creative in their use of this time, but a few ideas never hurt. The main suggestion is to do something for someone else. Put all that you would normally do one year into helping build a camp or creating a recreational area for an orphanage. Focus on specific persons or projects. Seeing your efforts change lives will bring considerably more joy than spending five hundred dollars to go somewhere fancy and learn how to lie in the sun.

A war correspondent tells a story of coming across a nun on her knees patiently swabbing the gangrenous leg of a very sick young soldier lying on a mat. Repulsed by the scene, he had to turn his head away. Finally he said to her, "Sister, I wouldn't do that for a million dollars."

The nun paused momentarily, and said, "Neither would I."

Some uses of our so-called free time transcend anything that money could buy.

Most people have pretty good handles on what might be considered normal-sized vacations, but are at a loss as to what to do with the little lumps of time. Hence, I'll skip over the family-size and the regular-size range and jump into mini, and two-minute vacations.

MINI-VACATIONS

Most of us fail to realize that we have built into our calendars fifty-two miniature vacations every year. With a little planning and creativity, these can be meaningful and joyful times.

The principle of one day out of every seven for worship and rest has been true since creation, but I know of very few people who take that commandment seriously. I still struggle with it. Again and again William McNamara's comments about learning how to "waste" that time for God's sake come back to haunt me. "There is only one way to truly celebrate the Sabbath— and that is to waste it prodigiously. Until I can waste time prodigiously I do not take God seriously. If Christ is real, He must be able to hold me and captivate me."[5] It is my acknowledgment of His sovereignty.

There must be a reason why rest was included in Creation, in the Ten Commandments, and why Jesus said that the Sabbath was made for man. There must be a reason why the Sabbath is fifty-two-times more important than any other "holy-day."

We need to break the habit of looking in the TV guide for our happiness each weekend. Plan some small trips where you drive less than two hours. Adopt the following three principles:

• Stay together
• Learn the flowers
• Travel lightly

Take as few "props" as possible. Also leave behind such excess baggage as worry, guilt, anxiety, and depression. Up your surprisability factor a couple notches and take off. My wife and I call it "Fresno-ing," because for a while our only vacations were mini ones, where we went into Fresno, got a motel—and just had the time of our lives doing simple things like going for a swim, going to a bookstore, taking in a movie, and having a quiet dinner together.

What about limiting your mini-vacation to one tank of gas—going anywhere you can and investing yourself as much as you can? What about a "one meal" vacation, meaning that you do what you can in your local area over a time period limited to one meal (you can go from right after breakfast until a late dinner, or longer if you discipline those hunger pangs). What about celebrating a Sunday by simply being alive to the leading of the Holy Spirit for a whole day? Itineraries are not allowed.

Have you ever had a "ludicrous Thursday lunch"? They were invented by a madcap genius friend of mine named Ray Rood. They can happen any day of the week, or even any time during the day, for that matter. Their singular purpose is to celebrate life with a little madness. Either spontaneous phone calls are made or formal invitations are sent out, designating a time and place. Meals are usually only a fabricated excuse to laugh at the funny things in life, especially in your own life. The atmosphere works almost like a magnet, drawing out the sad and difficult things into the light, and sharing them over a meal doused with laughter. The basic precept is that "if we don't all do something crazy, we might all go insane."

What about amplifying the meaning of a holiday with a little imagination, and then jumping in without a safety belt? On Valentine's Day one year, Zac, Joshua and I got up early, dressed up like Valentine Fairies (don't ask me what a Valentine Fairy looks like), cut out about two hundred little red hearts which we proceeded to place all over the house in the form of little "trails," and then we all went in and woke up mom. While she was following these strange trails all over the house, finding a little love-note or surprise at various junctions, Zac and I fixed a splendiferous "Breakfast for a Queen."

Some may say we're a little strange— but I'm beginning to realize that it might be a compliment. I'm not sure I want to be "normal" anymore. Some may think it's not worth the effort, but it would have been hard to convince Pam of that that morning (and us too).

I'm beginning to believe that God likes misfits. Christianity does not consist in abstaining from doing things no gentleman would think of doing, says R. L. Sheppard, but in doing things that are unlikely to occur to anyone who is not in touch with the Spirit of Christ.[6]

We have the power to convert any situation into a mission of gladness. Ben and Loretta Patterson told us recently of another incident in the life of their vibrant mother, who is now in her eighties. She was standing in a rather lengthy line waiting for some tickets. The line hadn't moved and the rain wouldn't stop. Rather than just be dismal, she asked someone to save her place in line for a few moments. A short time later she returned with thirty doughnuts, which she proceeded to give away to cheer everybody up. She had converted a rather dull moment into a magic one.

"The people around us can always read our hearts by our faces. The inner things we live with will always show up on our faces. The soul is dyed with the color of our com-

mitment. Our task is not to argue, philoso-
phize, speculate, cajole, but to live a life that
demands an explanation. Is there anything
about us that would force people to say,
'Now that's living! That's the way I wish I
could live!' A joy-filled life will always
demand an explanation—but too often we
want Life without having to change our life-
style."[7]

What about anniversaries? Do you
remember them? If you do, have you
bogged down to the same routine of dinner
and roses? Are you aware of the fact, for
example, that each year has a different
symbol—like the fifth year being wood,
and the ninth year being pottery? Do you
ever make something or find something to
commemorate these events? Or are you still
in too much of a hurry?

What about birthdays? Are parties
really just for kids? Don't tell my wife or
friends that—because this year they really
surprised me. Pam rented a whole room at
a restaurant and had friends come do a
"Tim Hansel Roast." I don't know who had
more fun, them or me.

We are surrounded with endless natural
occasions for joy if we would but take

advantage of them. What about making buttons this year to celebrate Columbus Day? Or be like Maureen Hoffman who even went so far as to celebrate "Garbage Day." She made special buttons to wear and share commemorating the men who work so hard to keep our cans empty. She even had buttons and signs for "One day after garbage day" and "Garbage day is only two days away." Now that's celebrating the ordinary.

MIDGET VACATIONS

Midget vacations fall along the same idea, but take even less time. We're called not only to structure sufficient time into each week for rest, recreation, and worship—but also into each day. Jim Carlson recently shared with me his idea for "a daily Sabbath." He said that if we're to tithe 10 percent of our energy and finances to the Lord, then shouldn't we do it with our time as well? Basically he said that 10 percent of each day would be 2.4 hours—and he's trying to develop the discipline that will allow him to creatively dedicate that time to knowing and enjoying God more.

Midget vacations open our eyes to all

that we have right at our feet, right in our own home. It might include trying to go outside every morning for a week and see something you've never seen before. Just because you've lived in the same house for twenty years doesn't mean you've seen everything.

Here are some other "morning midgets" you might want to try.

> • *Praise God for the sunrise (that means you have to be up to see it). I heard someone say that one of the greatest tragedies in the world today is that people no longer see the sunrise.*

> • *Don't get out of bed until you can think of one thing you're thankful for, and secondly, say, "This is the day that the Lord has made, let us rejoice and be glad" (and really mean it).*

> • *Go outside and yell (as loud as your inhibitions will allow), "Life, I love you!"*

> • *Hug something or someone.*

• *Instead of saying your normal grace before breakfast, either (a) sing a song, (b) whistle, (c) clap, or (d) just stomp your feet. In other words, praise him with your whole body, instead of just your lips.*

• *Phone somebody and wish them a happy day.*

• *Try to find something in your yard or house that you've never seen before. You'll be surprised at how many there are.*

• *Laugh at least once by the time breakfast is over.*

• *My father-in-law went to a seminar on goal setting, and he heard the speaker share a very unique goal: to be happy by eight o'clock. In other words, refuse to be controlled by your circumstances.*

• *Do something special for yourself in the morning—make yourself a special cup of tea, kiss your wife,* pat your dog, read a favorite section of Scripture. In other words, help yourself set the pace for the day.

• Smile at that face in the mirror and say, "I love you" (if you can't say that, then say, "Jesus loves you," because that's certainly true).

• Do something different in the morning. Put on two different color socks, wear tennis shoes with your suit, sit at a different chair at the breakfast table, write a poem, go to work in a different way this morning. Somehow break the normal routine of your morning.

• Tell each member of your family one reason why you're glad they're in your family.

• Tell Jesus one reason why you're glad he's your Lord.

• Think of five reasons you're glad that you're you, i.e., five things you like about yourself, and thank God.

• *Look around your house. I mean look around your house, and, before you leave for the day, think of one thing that you're grateful for. Don't forget it when you get caught up in that day's problems.*

• *Pray for someone. You'll be amazed at what it does for his or her life as well as for yours.*

• *Choose one word or one line of Scripture and follow it for the day. In other words, if you choose the word peace, or joy, or Lord, then really try and contemplate that all during the day. Write it down on scraps of paper so it'll remind you of something. Put it on your dash-board. Put it on your desk, but as much as you can during the day, try to make it a living reality in your life. Or choose a phrase such as* Patient endurance *and give the world living proof that Jesus is real in that way in your life. Or choose a sentence such as* No condemna-tion now hangs over the head of

those who are in Christ Jesus
(Rom. 8:1). *And remember that you
are free. Put flesh and bone on it.
Dance to its music. Celebrate its
reality. You will be amazed at how
different Scripture will become in
your life if you do this regularly.*

*• Make it a point to meet someone
new before lunchtime. You never
know what might happen.*

*• Phone your mate in the morning,
whether at the office or at home, and
just tell him or her how much you
love them. Have no other reason for
phoning, except to say how glad
you are that God chose them for you
to live out your life with.*

*• Thank someone who works at
your office, or who services your
home, for contributing to your life.
For example, thank that secretary
who answers all the phone calls. If
you get a chance, thank the garbage
man for picking up your garbage.
Stick a note on the mailbox for the*

mailman, just saying thanks for all the good news he brings each day. There are countless people in our lives to whom we forget to say thank you. This morning pick just one and tell him how much you appreciate him.

And what about the afternoon? Do you still subscribe to the notion that afternoons are "supposed" to be dull? I don't know who invented that myth, but he must be a millionaire by now because he has a lot of followers. (I think it was his brother who invented the one about Mondays.)

The afternoon often starts with lunch. Why not do something different today? Go to a different place to eat, or go to the same place, but with someone else.

> • *Tell the waitress that she's really doing a fine job, or leave her a note with your tip. Or really, I mean really, enjoy your food—focus in on it, taste it, explore it, instead of exploiting it. Take time to thank God for it. And if possible, try not to hurry through it.*

• *Go on a picnic during lunch. You might say, "That's impossible because I work downtown." Then sit on a park bench or a bench by the bus stop, and eat a sack lunch, and watch the people go by. It might give you a whole new perspective on life.*

• *Take a few minutes out of your lunch break to read a couple pages of something special—something that will inspire you to move into the afternoon with a little more power. It's a shame how frequently we exploit God's resources by being prejudiced against the afternoon (that is, in assuming we really can't get that much done in the after-noon). A friend told me that when he worked in Washington, D.C., he always had to get to people in the morning if he wanted to get some-thing done because they were usually so ineffective in the afternoon. Be different. Be His.*

Evening is really a special time of day. It's a time to relax, refocus. Time to be with your family. A time to think about what life is really all about. Hopefully, it's a time to be happy. Here are a couple of ideas to help cheer up your evening.

• Did you take any time to get some exercise today? One of the most important ways to stay alive and enjoy life is to get that oxygen and blood to pump through your body. If you haven't, go out for a short walk. Take someone from your family. Go for a little run if you can, or ride a bike. Jump rope or do something to make your heart beat.

• Help set the table in a different way tonight. Maybe you'll find some flowers in the yard and put them in the center. Maybe you'll make little name tags for everybody so they can sit down and make dinner look official and special. Maybe you'll put on some music that will help everybody relax. Maybe you'll get everybody to dress

up a little bit and help celebrate how very special eating together is.

• Have everyone share one thing they're thankful for at dinner. Again, gratitude is the basic attitude of happiness.

• Have someone different say grace tonight.

• If you want to try something really unusual, try eating with your opposite hand tonight. (It's also a good way to learn how to eat more slowly, which is a good way to cut down on some of your calorie intake.)

• Instead of your usual grace for meals, thank God for each thing on the table. When was the last time you thanked him for forks, knives, spoons, napkins, for salt or coffee? Learning to thank him for the little things creates a joyful heart.

• Have a gripe-and-appreciation

session during dinner. That means,
it's legal to share either a special
thing you appreciate about each
other or something you have
difficulty with. It does magical
things to open up conversation.

Are there minutes in your day that you could convert into vacations? Are you still, maybe even unknowingly, practicing being unhappy?

Sometimes life is not so much to be understood as it is to be lived out. Some of us spend more time analyzing life than we do living it. I need to remind you that joy is something you are. It's another way in which we express our gratitude for the one who lives within us and allow him to be expressed into a world that needs so many things. But it especially needs our grateful joy. I also need to remind all of us that it takes practice, practice, practice. Just like anything else, it will soon become a habit, and we can and will become contagiously happy.

The purpose of all this is to encourage you to both say and experience the words *Hallelujah . . . anyway.* Even if it's Monday.

Even if it's six-thirty in the morning. Even if your washer ate the socks again, for the third time this week. Even if your car died the week after your warranty expired. Even if your vacations are only fifteen minutes long these days.

Why spend so much energy "putting our lives back together"? Maybe this little story will be a good reminder. A father came home late one evening, exhausted. Heading for the easy chair, he picked up the evening paper, looking forward to a few moments' rest. No sooner had he hit the chair than his young son joined the newspaper on his lap. "Can we play, dad?"

The father loved his son very much but really felt he needed some time alone. Noticing a picture in the paper that evening from a recent moonprobe, he came up with a plan. It was a photo of the earth, taken from the moon. He cut the picture out and then cut it into small pieces, creating an instant jigsaw puzzle. Almost all the pieces looked alike. He encouraged his son to take it to his room with some tape and put the earth back together again.

The father was satisfied that he would have more than enough time to relax. He was quite surprised to see his son appear about ten minutes later—with the photograph of the earth intact.

"How did you do that so quickly?" he asked. "It was easy, dad," the boy replied. "There was a picture of a man on the back—and when I put the man together, the world came together."

Notes

1. Rosie Dosti, "Vacation Diet: Plan a Strategy," *Los Angeles Times*, June 8, 1978, p. 29.

2. Fynn, *Mister God, This is Anna* (New York: Ballantine books, 1974).

3. Mark Link, *Take Off Your Shoes*, (Niles, IL: Argus Communications, 1972), p. 110.

4. Ibid., p. 112.

5. William McNamara, *The Human Adventure* (Garden City, NY: Doubleday and Co., 1974), p. 74.

6. Lloyd Ogilvie, *Drumbeat of Love* (Waco, TX: Word Books, 1976), p. 112.

7. Ibid, p. 108.

Helping Families Grow Series

❦ *Communicating Spiritual Values Through Christian Music*

❦ *Equipping Your Child for Spiritual Warfare*

❦ *Family Vacations That Work*

❦ *Helping Your Child Stand Up to Peer Pressure*

❦ *How to Discover Your Child's Unique Gifts*

❦ *How to Work With Your Child's Teachers*

❦ *Helping Your Child Love to Read*

❦ *Improving Your Child's Self-Image*

❦ *Preparing for Your New Baby*

❦ *Should My Child Listen to Rock Music?*

❦ *Spiritual Growth Begins at Home*

❦ *Surviving the Terrible Teenage Years*

ABOUT THE AUTHOR

Tim Hansel is a popular speaker and bestselling author. His previous books for adults include *Eating Problems for breakfast, Holy Sweat, What Kids Need Most in a Dad, When I Relax I Feel Guilty, You Gotta Keep Dancin'*, and the recently released *Through the Wilderness of Loneliness*.

Tim is the founder of Summit Expedition, a wilderness survival school and ministry. He also serves as Vice President of Communication Resources for World Servants, a program that provides organization with incredible short term mission opportunities around the world.

Tim lives in Southern California with his wife, Pam, and their sons, Zac and Josh.